Sponsor

Acknowledgments

I want to give a special thanks to everyone who helped me with the process of writing this book, whether it was giving money, a listening ear, offering a critique, or giving me knowledge of the self-publishing process.

So let me start my list by thanking my big brother Sa-eed, aka Happy, for always supporting me and also for his monetary contribution.

Secondly, I want to thank my friend Donte for his monetary support of the book.

I also want to thank Simon for his monetary support of the book.

I would also like to thank someone who played a very important role in the book, A'zarria Sanford, for doing some of the editing and creating the book cover that you guys love. If you want to contact her for designs, her Instagram is @majorstar.designs.

The next list of people I'm going to name are those who gave me insight and feedback on the book, starting with a great friend of mine named Fonzo. He has actually critiqued my poetry since I started writing poetry three years ago. He has listened, critiqued, and given me feedback every step of the way in the process of the book.

Secondly, I would like to thank my beautiful daughter Daliyah for supporting all of my projects and giving me her feedback and thoughts on the book.

Thirdly, I would like to thank my friend Shawnta. She always picks up her phone no matter what time it is, even if it's 3 am. Thank you for always being available and willing to listen.

I would also like to thank a good friend of mine, Tesha Finley, for her listening ears and for giving me insight on self-publishing.

Last but not least, I would like to thank this, great comedian, and a great friend, Michael Colyar, for his continuous push, for me to write a book and for all the opportunities he has given me.

Additionally, I would like to thank anybody who has liked, suggested, and purchased this book.

And most of all, I would like to thank the Most High.

A little about the author

Kamal Braddox, also known as Kamal Speaks, is a truly inspiring figure in the world of poetry. Despite experiencing a difficult setback where he lost what he thought was everything, he managed to find a new beginning through his art even when faced with homelessness. It's incredible how life can lead us down unexpected paths, and Kamal's journey showcases the resilience and creativity of the human spirit.

In the face of adversity, Kamal discovered his passion for poetry and used it as a means of self-expression and healing. His words became a powerful tool for him to navigate through challenging times. It's a testament to his strength and determination that he was able to turn his life around and become a world-renowned poet.

Kamal's story serves as a reminder that our circumstances don't define us, but rather it's our choices and actions that shape our lives. Despite hitting rock bottom, he found the courage to pursue his passion and ultimately found success. His journey is a true inspiration for anyone facing difficulties or feeling lost, reminding us that there is always hope and a way to reinvent ourselves.

If you have any more questions or need further assistance, feel free to ask!

INSTAGRAM KamalSpeaks1

YOUTUBE KamalSpeaks1

TIK TOK KamalSpeaks1

EMAIL KamalSpeaks57@gmail.com

FACEBOOK KamalSpeaks1

Contents

Sponsor I
Acknowledgments II
A little about the author V
Introduction X
The Story Behind Poverty Poem 1
    POVERTY POEM 3
        THOUGHTS OF A POEM 5
The Story Behind Fighting For My Soul Poem 6
    FIGHTING FOR MY SOUL POEM 8
        THOUGHTS OF A POEM 10
The Story Behind Helping Hand Poem 11
    HELPING HAND POEM 14
        THOUGHTS OF A POEM 16
The Story Behind Currency Poem 17
    CURRENCY POEM 19
        THOUGHTS OF A POEM 21
The Story Behind God bless The Child 22
    GOD BLESS THE CHILD POEM 24
        THOUGHTS OF A POEM 26
The Story Behind I Inspire Change 27
    I INSPIRE CHANGE POEM 29
        THOUGHTS OF A POEM 30
The Story Behind Yelle Poem 31
    YELLE POEM 33

THOUGHTS OF A POEM	34
The Story Behind Homeless Love	35
HOMELESS LOVE POEM	36
THOUGHTS OF A POEM	39
The Story Behind Melanin Goddess	40
MELANIN GODDESS POEM	42
THOUGHTS OF A POEM	44
The Story Behind Jasmine's Poem	45
JASMINE'S POEM	47
THOUGHTS OF A POEM	49
The Story Behind Love Boat poem	50
LOVE BOAT POEM	53
THOUGHTS OF A POEM	55
The Story Behind Inner Beauty Poem	56
INNER BEAUTY POEM	58
THOUGHTS OF A POEM	60
The Story Behind Rinse Cycle Poem	61
RINSE CYCLE POEM	64
THOUGHTS OF A POEM	66
The Story Behind Gate Keepers Poem	67
GATE KEEPERS POEM	70
THOUGHTS OF A POEM	73
The Story Behind Walking Dead Poem	74
WALKING DEAD POEM	76
THOUGHTS OF A POEM	78

The Story Behind God's Words Poem 79
    GODS WORDS POEM 81
        THOUGHTS OF A POEM 83
The Story Behind Manifestation Poem 84
    MANIFESTATION POEM 86
        THOUGHTS OF A POEM 88
The reason for the story and what was happening while the story was being told 89
Sneak peek introduction the sequel 96

Introduction

This book is not just an assortment of poems and short stories; it is a reflection of who I am. My poetry is a response to life, a snapshot of my experiences captured in verse. As you delve into the seventeen poems within these pages, you'll also journey into seventeen accompanying short stories that birthed them. It's as if you're stepping into my shoes, penning each verse and living each tale yourself. This collection is designed to keep you captivated, to keep you on the edge, eagerly awaiting the next story, the next poem. So, strap in, we're about to take off into a whirlwind of emotions, experiences, and revelations. And remember, there's a bonus story at the end, a tale that just might transform your life. I hope you'll stay with me for the ride.

The story behind Poverty poem

Poverty! This poem is intriguing, especially in how it originated. I recall sitting in my van, the very van I was living in at that time. The opening verse came to me. "I speak the language of pain and anguish." I repeated this line over and over, feeling its power. I didn't know where the poem was heading, but I wondered what's the language of pain and anguish while sitting in my van, surrounded by all of my belongings, with only two dollars to my name, with a broken air conditioner making it hot, muggy, and hunger getting the best of me.

As I look at all of these circumstances and repeated that verse, it struck me like a ton of bricks – poverty! The first step I took was to dive into the various forms of poverty, not just my own. Once I had researched it thoroughly, I chose to speak as if I were poverty itself, embodying its very essence. Poverty is a situation, a mindset. It does not define who you truly are unless you allow it to.

POVERTY POEM

I speak the language, of pain and anguish.

__I am poverty !__

I have a sign that says can you spare a dime?

You laugh at me but you don't know this life of mines.

__I am poverty !__

I don't know if you notice , but they gave me six feet before Covid.

I am poverty, and society starving me.

I'm a military veteran, misguided adolescent.

I'm hungers true essence.

I'm an ex millionaire.

A mother without a job who cares,

__I am poverty !__

I'm a child at night that's afraid of the light.

I'm a father who's bothered when his children awakened, and haven't eaten.

__I am poverty !__

And the funny thing is ya'll don't understand the pain I bring.

I mess up Families destroy neighborhoods.

I'm a curse. The worst, the reverse,

steal from the poor give to the rich Robin Hood.

I'm under investigation for homicide, the gentle whispers in suicide.

I'm a plague on this earth I'm a genocide.

I'm What's wrong When momma has her soft cry.

I'm grand larceny, armed robbery.

Oh yeah it's a pleasure to meet you.

I am poverty !

Traditional punctuations are not used. Author wants you to read the poem as if he was saying it

THOUGHTS OF A POEM

Hopefully you were inspired to write your thoughts or a poem so here's a space for you.

The story behind fighting for my Soul poem

This poem, this poem right here, hits me hard because it shows my transition from worldly to spiritual. It came at a time when I felt like I was losing everything, especially my money (lol). It's amusing how we tend to attribute everything to money.

So, I was losing my money while simultaneously dealing with a false accusation from a young lady in the court system. I faced the possibility of losing my freedom, or what I perceived as freedom. I was already locked up, thinking that financial freedom held more importance than spiritual freedom. When you forget about the Most High, you will always be reminded of the devil. In a world controlled by temptation, we often find ourselves worshipping cars, clothes, money, sex, and drugs. It's a battle, no! It's a war. You have to fight for your soul every day. That's precisely what I did, and continue to do. There's a question I'm ask continuously about a line in this poem. The line. I turned to my sister who was a soldier and told her this will be the coldest summer ever. I was referring to sister soldier and her book the coldest winter ever.

FIGHTING FOR MY SOUL POEM

My mind was closed eyes shut,

prayed for guidance now my soul is opening up.

From an abyss that was dark and empty.

Found out that lust turns into envy,

greed rages into hatred. Congratulations you took the red pill now you're in the matrix.

Caught in mixture of two worlds.

Seduction Strong enough to make a man believe he's a girl.

Or a woman to say she's a dad.

Wait a minute is that the son I never had.

We worship the material.

Give me a second. Let me tell you about my scenario.

I wanted to drive the luxury cars.

Live in the luxury spots.

Was fening for the Rolex, but when I put it on it felt like a regular watch.

At that moment time stopped.

I was worshiping, the worst within.

And if I didn't change, I'd be cursed again.

I had pledge allegiance, to egregious life.

Got on one knee proposed took the devil As my wife.

At that moment came the lightning and the thunder. turned to my sister, who was a soldier, and told her,

this would be the coldest summer, ever!

Did you peep the metaphor clever.

If you didn't get it, just forget it.

Back to the subject at hand.

Lust and greed turned me into a toxic man.

Couldn't breathe George Floyd needed oxygen.

Trapped in myself I was boxed within.

I woke to charges of woman abuse, lies mixed with truth,

and all the money in the world couldn't help me.

They wanted to destroy me cause they thought I was young black and wealthy.

But what they didn't know my mind wasn't healthy.

And all this came about when I prayed to God to help me.

He said son you got to be patient.

You must be strong prepare your soul for temptation.

And as I crossed into light from the dark,

the devil said umm wait a minute remember you said to death do us part.

And I'm still fighting for my soul.

Traditional punctuations are not used. Author wants you to read the poem as if he was saying it

THOUGHTS OF A POEM

Hopefully you were inspired to write your thoughts or a poem so here's a space for you.

The Story Behind Helping hand poem

The poem "Helping Hand" was born out of a difficult period in my life. I had experienced financial loss, false charges that could have led to years in prison, and homelessness. I was forced to sleep in my van, and the hardest part was not receiving the support I needed from my family. Family has always been incredibly important to me, and I have always gone above and beyond to help them in any way I could – whether it was assisting with moving, paying rent, lending clothes, buying clothes, or helping them find employment or start a business. I was always there, even if it meant getting physically involved.

It was devastating to realize that I couldn't receive the same level of help from my family when I needed it the most. For example, when I first started my poetry career, I reached out to my mother, father, brother, and sisters for feedback on my poems. Unfortunately, the response was minimal, and what little feedback I did receive was mostly negative. My younger brother, who is just one year younger than me, even told me that he couldn't listen to my poetry because it didn't feel like me. It struck me as a bold and ignorant statement because how could he know if it was me or not if he didn't even give it a chance? It's worth mentioning that I had been a devoted supporter of his rap career, attending all his shows, listening to his music, and providing honest feedback. Help isn't just about financial assistance; it can also come in the form of kind words and a listening ear. Support can take many different forms. Instead of uplifting me, my family spoke negatively to me. The minimal help I did receive, which I appreciated, was talk about and shared with the world.

When I asked for a loan to get back on my feet, one family member responded by saying, "If the bank won't give it to you, why should I?" It's important to note that I wasn't struggling with substance abuse or continuously getting in trouble with the law. My family had witnessed my success and the millions I had made in my previous career. Unfortunately, all my troubles seemed to happen at once.

Observing how my family treated me and witnessing how we, as a people, treat each other made me realize how flawed our teachings are. We are taught to get it out the mud, meaning not to ask. We discourage asking for help and view it as a sign of weakness, when in reality, supporting and helping one another is the ultimate display of strength. This realization compelled me to write this poem – it was a burning desire within me that I had to release. Despite everything that transpired between my family and me, I still love them, and I believe they love me too. We simply need to learn how to love each other better.

HELPING HAND POEM

A helping hand!
to degrade and belittle is that really helping that man?
A helping hand!
taking shots at my dignity, broadcasting my business telling everybody what you did for me.
A helping hand!
Helping me just enough not to get up, we call that a sit up,
A helping hand!
This behavior was taught by our enslaver, we was tricked and led to believe that a white Jesus would be our savior.
And the Willie Lynch letters made us, hate us, and television and radio kept the hate up.
So have you, subconsciously we treat each other like crabs in a barrel.
When the gun aimed at me, it's really pointing at you, and the media saying look at what black versus black do .
And Karen's on the phone saying yeah it's a black dude.
I don't sympathize. I empathize,
how can we still fall for these lies.
That's so many years old. How can you kill a nation's soul?
We can remember 12 years of slavery, but forget centuries worth of bravery.

That amazes me.

And amazingly, we could protest the police but not speak out against what's plain to see.

Guess that's how we trained to be.

So in this situation, Division is more than math.

Give me a second there's more to grasp.

That's why we afraid to ask.

Cause we are here more than laughs.

So before attacking one another, sister and brother, before slapping them, let me give you a acronym.

Help *Higher Elevation Love and Patience.*

You'd be surprised what that'll do for our situation.

Where one and the same so when you help me it's self preservation.

Instead we take the Lauren Hill miseducation,

and that's what we don't understand, that unity is the first stand.

Forget the name Adam and Eve because melanin was the first man.

I love you and I give you my heart. An exchange for a genuine helping hand.

Traditional punctuations are not used. Author wants you to read the poem as if he was saying it

THOUGHTS OF A POEM

Hopefully you were inspired to write your thoughts or a poem so here's a space for you.

The Story Behind Currency Poem

This is one of my favorite poems. It's a reminder that money is man-made. The majority of every symbol on it represents something evil. We give money power. For a long time, I believed having money gave me power so, to make a long story short, I went to Texas to help some old friends with their business; a business I was once in and highly skilled at.

Ninety-eight percent of the conversation I heard while I was out there was about money. It was more important than their family, friends, health, and in most cases, even God. It was a no-brainer; I had to write a poem about it. I decided for this poem to embody money and speak as if money itself was talking to them, like I did in the poverty poem. So, I studied all the symbols on the dollar bill and got to work. Through observation, study, and my personal belief in what's important to me, and the connection to my spiritual side, a masterpiece was born.

CURRENCY POEM

Currently, I'm your currency.

You can call me dollar last name Bill.

I could change the way you feel.

Give a ugly person sex appeal.

See the game change when it's no change involved.

Many believe in me more than they believe in God.

Keep in mind, I was designed, to steal your peace of mind, so you could have a piece of mines,

That almighty, them bills you grip so tightly. You know what excites me,

Is I can have you sell your soul, make a woman unrobe, convince a man to put on woman's clothes.

I'm the reason you get married and divorce, so powerful The courts named me child support.

Cause I take care of this great nation full of many men, who would do anything to be my friend.

It started with Benjamin Franklin, You can thank, him,

and his compadres for taking what you need, trees, to make me forget if you breathe,

As long as you use your last breath, to figure out where I go next.

They say I'm the root of all evil.

Too much of me is lethal.

I'm bad for your health.

But what's wrong with generational wealth?

You see how many I help.

The Waltons, the Rockefellers, the Roth Childs.

Oh yeah, that's it.

Only the 1%.

And that includes all your presidents, but that's irrelevant.

What's important, is the assortment, of pictures, and scriptures,

That make my anatomy, that steals your soul gradually. or should I say magically,

Because I'm printed from thin air.

So now you know the cost, but unfortunately you're day late and a dollar short.

Traditional punctuations are not used. Author wants you to read the poem as if he was saying it

THOUGHTS OF A POEM

Hopefully you were inspired to write your thoughts or a poem so here's a space for you.

The story behind God bless the child

The poem "God Bless the Child" hits you in the gut, whether you're considering it from the eyes of a child or as a parent. From both perspectives, it's a stark reminder of the brutal cycle in our melanin-rich community, a cycle that was triggered and continues to be driven by exterior forces, but we are the ones who keep it going. It's our community where the drama of baby mama and baby daddy is so common it's seen as normal. We're conditioned to despise each other, during and after our relationships. It's not a coincidence, it's a setup, but we are the ones who keep falling for the trap.

I grew up in the midst of my parents' toxic relationship. Their own emotions and conflicts overshadowed their responsibilities - us, their kids. It felt like they vented their relationship frustrations on me. I remember this one time when I was ten, my dad took me and my little brother on a trip to Georgia. On the way, I told him about a hole in my sneaker and asked if he could buy me a new pair. He looked me dead in the eyes and said, "Hell no! I ain't buying you nothing, I pay your mother child support. Ask her!" I had to swallow back the tears. There are more stories, believe me, they only get worse.

Fast forward to my own daughters and the relationship I had with their mother. It was toxic when we were together, and I won't lay all the blame on her. I had a part in it too. But when we broke up, or rather when she dumped me and I didn't want to return to the relationship after she wanted me back, our children became casualties of war. She'd move constantly to keep the kids away from me. Told them to run if they saw me, saying I would kidnap them. God only knows what else she filled their heads with. When I asked her why she was doing this, she said if I couldn't love her, there was no way I could love our children. After a couple of years, I won custody of my girls, but the damage was done. The sad part is that this is not a unique story. We lack emotional intelligence and self-awareness, keeping us in this destructive cycle. The moment we put our children first, is the moment our situation will start to change.

GOD BLESS THE CHILD POEM

Cries ' of a young child

from confusion, of an illusion,

of a life they should have had.

Faced with the harsh realities of growing up in a cruel world without a dad.

Switch to a mother's point of view, she's not really thinking when she says she hates daddy in front of you,

or maybe she is, and her plan for payback is the kids.

Cries, from a father when he looks in his

daughter's eyes, and she looks back with

hatred because her head is filled with her mother's lies.

Caught in the crossfire, of the parents' lust greed and desire,

for one another. Or maybe it's one and not the other.

Father refuses to see child because he can't have a relationship with the mother.

She goes to court, for child support, but that baby don't want money It's more concerned about the parent that's lost,

cries itself to sleep at night. Wounds hit heavy cut deep like a knife.

Doctor says no need for surgery that child is scarred for life.

So its a couple of things we must consider, before ruining someone's life because our love lives are bitter.

Taking relationship advice from Facebook and Twitter, using the television to be our kids babysitter.

I'm gonna end it like this. I want all my children to put their hands in the air make a fist,

and tell your parents that your lives are ours.

Good parenting is the first step to black power.

Traditional punctuations are not used. Author wants you to read the poem as if he was saying it

THOUGHTS OF A POEM

Hopefully you were inspired to write your thoughts or a poem so here's a space for you.

The Story Behind I inspire change

I inspire change poem has a very interesting story behind it. I was hired by a young lady who owned a brand called "I inspire change." Well, I wouldn't say hired because she never paid me for the poem, so I kept it. In no way, shape, or form am I throwing shade on her. She's a very beautiful woman with a great brand, and I believe she has a good heart. But moving on, this poem was me expressing what it took for me to get out of that dark place I was in. In order to move to the next level in life, no matter where it is, the first step is to change; whether it is changing your surroundings, changing people, changing habits, or changing the way you think, change must come.

Now let me give you the back end of the story; I'm a full-time poet, meaning all of my income comes from selling my merch and performing at shows, but more so from selling merch because I was doing a lot of shows for free; building a name.

The merch I was selling was my shirts and hats, but due to inflation, a major inflation, I couldn't afford to get my next shipment of merch. So I had to make a change. I hope y'all caught that, i.e., "Change," the name of the poem l.o.l. So I had an associate of mine put a picture behind the poem, and I brought some picture frames and sold that as merch. Doing that paid all of my bills. Positive change is always good.

I INSPIRE CHANGE POEM

Longing to be different. Searching for what my gift is,

knowing things can't stay the same.

I inspire change.

With none to spare, eliminate doubt and fear.

Campaigning for a better me, for a future I can barely see,

but I know it's brighter, because faith is my lighter,

and I'm burning all bridges.

That leads, to false thoughts and insecurities, in search of a purer me.

Because I am the reflection of perfection.

With God's protection, I have a holy erection.

That means I stand straight, and with faith,

I can walk through burning lakes,

of fire. I inspire,

health wealth, and with the help, of the most high and within his name I inspire change.

Traditional punctuations are not used. Author wants you to read the poem as if he was saying it

THOUGHTS OF A POEM

Hopefully you were inspired to write your thoughts or a poem so here's a space for you.

The story behind Yelle poem

This poem was inspired by my encounter with Yandy Smith Harris, who some of you may recognize from the TV show Love and Hip-Hop. As a full-time poet, my days are filled with selling my merchandise and performing at night. One of my regular stops was a barbershop called "Legends" in ATL, where talented barbers like Q and Ed worked. Every time I performed there and sold my merchandise, people would suggest that I go up the block to Yandy's store and share my poetry with her. At the time, I wasn't familiar with who she was because I didn't watch the show. Eventually, I took their advice and went to her store, where she happened to be that day. She had a good number of customers there, about nine or ten. I asked her if I could share my poetry with her and her customers, and she graciously agreed. That was the beginning of a meaningful friendship.

Yandy has supported me in every possible way, from giving me opportunities to perform on stage to being a part of my movie. But more importantly, she has always been kind and uplifting, especially during times when I felt alone. She never expected anything in return, except for me to pay it forward and help others when I could. She is truly a beautiful soul. I also can't forget to mention her lovely mother, Laura, who often accompanies me on walks and helped inspire part of the title for this book.

After all that Yandy has done for me, I was eager to find a way to repay her. But how do you give something to someone who seems to have everything? The answer came to me: a poem. It reminded me of where we first met, at her store called Yelle Skin Care. Her products are all-natural and work wonders for the skin. I was excited to write this poem, making sure it embodied the same natural and pure qualities as her skincare line.

By the way, if you ever find yourself in Atlanta, I highly recommend visiting her store. And if that's not possible, you can always order her products online.

YELLE POEM

They say beauty is only skin deep, but what about when your skin ain't deep, enough.

Rough, dry, covered in hives?

Now you gotta apologize.

Makeup, with make up, beat your face up.

But the camouflage, is truly the sabotage, of your avatar.

See, the face, reacts better to chemicals that's plant-based.

So no need to scream and yell.

Instead use yelle, You'd be surprised how it makes your skin feel.

It repairs skin cells.

So take a chance at romance.

Fall in love with yourself again, become your own best friend.

But remember it starts with your skin.

Traditional punctuations are not used. Author wants you to read the poem as if he was saying it

THOUGHTS OF A POEM

Hopefully you were inspired to write your thoughts or a poem so here's a space for you.

The Story Behind Homeless Love

The story behind this poem is rooted in self-reflection and healing. After looking back at all of my intimate relationships, I was forced to confront my wrongdoings. Growing up, I had been taught by society that a man shows his manhood by sleeping with as many women as possible and making the most money. However, once I realized that money was fake and an orgasm only lasted 15 seconds, but love lasted forever, my outlook changed drastically.

With my newfound perspective, I found myself ready to love again, but with no one to love. It was as if I was homeless, as if I had no place to call home. That is when I realized that giving your heart to the right woman represents always having somewhere to live because your love will always live in her heart. And so, I used this concept of a home as a metaphor for the woman in this poem.

HOMELESS LOVE POEM

20 below, high windshield plus snow,

harsh weather. Whether, I got a place to stay or not.

See this thing called love.

It's tough without a home, forced to live in these mean streets, of mistakes.

Heartaches, the heartaches,

for a place to call home. But a house is not a home.

Luther Vandross.

But what about when you don't have an apartment, to start with?

Forced to live in darkness.

Can't see no food, nothing to eat.

But there's an ice box where my heart used to be.

Forced to eat out of a dumpster Of Regrets, reminiscing about all the beautiful houses I had and are there any left?

See the situations I left. Went left,

because I wasn't right. But who's to say who was wrong?

Did I lose everything because I was so strong?

See pride, can divide, and hide, true emotions, which is needed to pay rent.

To be honest with your feelings is money well spent.

late night fishing expeditions, took me from home cooked meals to eating outta soup kitchens, souped off of what I was missing.

A hard head makes a soft a** when you don't listen.

My friends would tell me I had a beautiful home that I took for granted.

Abandoned, damage demanded,

too much, when she was already enough, but she said enough, was enough.

So I had to find shelter, at a homeless shelter, to shelter, my feelings.

It was either that or sleep outside where there was no walls or ceilings.

Where everybody could see me. My feelings on display like 3d,

and they laughed at my pain, as I begged for spare change,

of love and affection. How did I get here?

I had a promising career,

and a nice house, but a house is not a home.

And I didn't figure that out until I was all alone.

THOUGHTS OF A POEM

Hopefully you were inspired to write your thoughts or a poem so here's a space for you.

The story behind melanin goddess

I was inspired to write this poem because of a friend of mine. She's a remarkable poet out of Chicago. Let me start by saying her physical appearance was amazing; she was truly beautiful, but she didn't think this of herself in my opinion. I would hear it in our conversations that she didn't see or forget how beautiful she was, as most of my melanin goddesses tend not to see this beauty they possess.

I wrote this poem as a reminder to them that they are worth more than gold. They are priceless and can't be purchased. Your beauty goes beyond the skin. You're a matrix of complex components that make up the beautiful melanin goddess you are, and I couldn't imagine life without you; for that, I will always love you.

I wanted to point out something, a line in this poem that I think people miss or just can't put together. The part when I say you must know her ark because once that ship has sailed, was a play on words.

Her ark, in comparison to Noah's ark, symbolizes the melanin women as humanity's salvation, and her ark, which is the womb, is what carries life. So fellas, you don't want to miss this ride, and this is a ship you need to honor.

MELANIN GODDESS POEM

Her words are timeless so forget the hourglass.
She can make an hour last.
A day, maybe a week.
That means thoughts of her remain after we speak.
Her wellbeing, is my purpose of being.
She's been blessed with a gift to prophesize.
To see the world through a prophet's eyes, she inhales the pain of humanity and make her words cry.
You could see it through a bird's eye, view.
Many will come but few are chosen, clothed in,
royalties attire, the robes of the true Messiah's,
dressed in a gods body. Instead of trying to ravage her body,
I need to get to know her soul, her goals, her deepest thoughts her worries, that past she's trying to bury.
She doesn't need to be convinced of her confidence.
She just needs a shoulder to cry on, a friend to rely on.
She just needs what she gives fare Exchanges is no robbery, but Larceny, of the heart, is dark,
she's biblical so you must know her ark.
Cause once that ship has sailed, all attempts will fail, at getting her back, when she just needs you to have her back.

See her beauty will catch the eyes of all men.

She's a Goddess so she's free of all sin.

She just needs a God that's all in.

the law of attraction, is action, that matches,

one another.

So Hopefully the God in me, matches the God in she.

And This is not a love Jones this is a love joined through poetry

Traditional punctuations are not used. Author wants you to read the poem as if he was saying it

THOUGHTS OF A POEM

Hopefully you were inspired to write your thoughts or a poem so here's a space for you.

The Story Behind Jasmine's Poem

This piece of writing, initially, was my first venture into creating a uplifting feel good poem. I recall someone remarking on how they appreciated my poetry, particularly the way I touched on subjects that needed attention, even though my work often had a dark tone. That inspired me to write Jasmine.

Jasmine was meant to be a poem about my process of writing poetry. However, things took a different turn when I met a woman named Jasmine. She was remarkable— bright, gorgeous, benevolent, and possessed a strength that was gentle and soft. She was poetry personified. So, instead of being a poem about my writing process, it became a reflection of my feelings towards poetry, symbolized by Jasmine.

Sadly, Jasmine and I never ended up together. But on a brighter note, I found a lifelong partner in poetry. The original intent behind this poem was to provide an insight into how I craft my poems. But in the process, I ended up teaching myself about my unique writing style, which revolves around the expression of emotions.

JASMINE'S POEM

Pain and hurt. I ain't gonna lie that's when I do some of my best work.

Write a piece to make my ex flirt.

My pen is hungry so I have to feed it.

I never understand victory until I truly learn what defeat is.

Trials and tribulations.

The workshop for discipline and patience.

Word rehabilitation.

Use my pen to create a situation.

Not to mention divine intervention.

I met a queen whose intellect caught my attention.

It wasn't her outer beauty, it was her inner source.

Our conversation was like erotic intercourse.

But of course, these words can't be forced.

When come to writing a poem it must take its natural course.

What's lost, will be found.

Verbs and pronouns, Floetry and sound.

No capping.

The smallest thing could insight a poem like the Sweet Smell of Jasmine, a foreign accent, world events, or using the world to event.

But back to Jasmine and that amazing scent.

See what inspires, could be one's wildest desires, burned through your soul like LA and a thousand brush fires.

And when that fire, is transferred to the sheet, transform into speech, spoken word is born.

I guess what I'm trying to say, is put feelings behind whatever you're trying to say.

Your inspiration could be bigger or smaller.

Mines is Jasmine, so that's what I choose to call her.

So Jasmine, or should I say poetry?

You know its' the spoken truth when Kamal speaks poetry.

Traditional punctuations are not used. Author wants you to read the poem as if he was saying it

THOUGHTS OF A POEM

Hopefully you were inspired to write your thoughts or a poem so here's a space for you.

The Story Behind Love Boat poem

This poem actually started as a challenge. I was having a conversation with a female poet about relationships, and during this conversation, she asked me to hear a poem she just wrote. Her poem was about a bad relationship and she did it in a basic way. Don't get it twisted, her poetry is great, her wordplay is phenomenal, but this particular poem was basic. So, I challenged her to write a poem about relationships using nothing but ships as her analogies and metaphors.

As I'm giving her the assignment, I thought to myself, "This is dope!" And I told her, "Forget it, I am going to do it." But I let her know that if she wanted, she could write her own version. I got to work immediately. My first steps were to look back at all my past relationships and then look at what I perceive to be healthy relationships and compare the two.

What I gathered was, I've moved too quickly in certain relationships and I didn't take the time to get to know the person. I skipped right past the friendship, straight to a relationship, which many of us do. We let the flesh cloud our judgment and block the words coming from our souls. A person will tell you everything you need to know about them without you asking. Spending time with them will give you opportunities for situations to happen, this will reveal their true character. It's very important to become a friend first. My past intentions when meeting these women was to have sex, so after that mission was completed, there was nothing to fall back on. We had no bond, nothing keeping us together. What starts off wrong ends off wrong.

Another thing, lack of communication. How can we expect commitment without communication? And arguing is not communicating. This is where the partnership comes into place. Understanding that we both have something equally important to say, and we need to work together to understand each other.

So, in my personal opinion, there are three ships you must ride to get to the promise land of love. And they go in this specific order: first, you must develop a friendship. Second, you must communicate and agree to a partnership. Third, you must trust the process of the relationship.

So, there you have it. This is why I chose to set the poem up the way I did. All aboard the love boat, we're taking a forever journey into the deep blue sea of love.

LOVE BOAT POEM

Pardon me for violating your personal space, but I wanna invite you to a private place.

So this conversation can't wait.

I want to take you on a trip, but first I'm gonna need you to board my friendship,

not relations. Its' says friends and its' is docked and waiting.

And the port reads patience.

But I'm gonna need you to leave your baggage because it may cause you to overthink, which can cause the ship to sink.

So exhale, as we take sail,

and I'm not sure of our final destination, but I know the strength of the ship will be tested by situations,

and the answer, might be a transfer.

So all aboard, as we travel all abroad, and explore,

this friendship, which then turns into a partnership.

See, I don't work for you. You don't work for me.

We work together to navigate through the sea.

There'll be idle days, tidal waves, nice days, where you can sunbathe.

In other words, as long as the ship stays strong, we could weather any storm,

This boat ride, will create a soul tie.

Without us even knowing this partnership, will turn into a relationship.

And on this ship, money is not an urgency, because our love or shall I say, this ship will flow with the currency.

So as I approach land, a married man, greeted by the sands,

of time, from a divine, adventure, where experience has been our mentor,

I want to thank you for trusting the process.

Understanding that relations can't come before friends, and a good partnership never ends.

Is funny how we're back where we begin, but now can say I love you to my best friend.

Traditional punctuations are not used. Author wants you to read the poem as if he was saying it

THOUGHTS OF A POEM

Hopefully you were inspired to write your thoughts or a poem so here's a space for you.

The Story Behind inner beauty poem

This one right here came to me right after being verbally assaulted on my Instagram Live by 27 melanin women because I expressed my notion that I don't like women to wear makeup. Let me be completely honest, ladies, most men don't like makeup. Please don't be confused; just because we tolerate it doesn't mean we like it. I can safely say all men hate the use of fake eyelashes (LOL).

I've had a couple of women tell me that they know they look better without the makeup, and they are aware men don't like it. When asked why do they wear it knowing this? The common answer given is that they do it for themselves. The first time I heard this reply, I was confused, but now I understand. The pressure of social norms and our identity being stripped away is why our melanin women feel they need to look a certain way other than their natural selves.

Let me give you an example. I was at Walmart in line to pay for my items, in front of me was a white woman, and I remember looking at her hair and thinking to myself, it just lay there lifeless, and visions of my melanin women's hair came to my mind. I thought of how full of life it was, and how it stood like a crown. At that moment, I started to look around and noticed all of the melanin women in Walmart that day had wigs on. The same as the white woman's hair. It was mind-blowing.

Men play a role in it too, using myself as an example. Before my epiphany, I would only date women with big butts, I was attracted to women who walk around half-naked. But when you have a misguided sense of morals, this is what you attract, and that's just what I got. I don't want any confusion, now I'm more into the spiritual connection rather than the physical. But being comfortable with your natural physical is part of your spiritual journey, in my personal opinion.

This poem was designed to manifest my wife and to remind my melanin women they are beautiful just the way they are. Your soul doesn't need to wear a wig, and your spirit self doesn't need makeup.

INNER BEAUTY POEM

Let me paint the picture of my ideal woman.
Not perfect, cause only God is perfect.
It's just my job to scratch the surface.
So we'll start with her feet.
What lies beneath, she would rule and they need not look no certain way as long as her souls, match her soul, and she's ready for this soul, journey.
Her spirit is what concerns me.
So can we walk for a minute?
My driver's license suspended or my car ain't been invented.
That takes me to your hands. Are you willing to build with this man?
Baked from scratch?
Rub my back.
When society has placed its weight on my shoulders, can you paint that picture?
I'm looking for a shapeshifter.
Someone who can go from hood to scripture, so what that mouth do.
Can you say your prayers in Hebrew.
Cause I don't want to hear no evil.
Speak life into me,
and through your eyes I can see, I'm where I'm supposed to be.

Your vision, is my circumcision.

So my manhood is good.

And with your sight of what lies ahead, is better than head.

So let's deal with your mind instead.

I love a woman who thinks before she talks, thinks about her thoughts, thinks like a boss, but of course,

thinks enough to listen.

Her ears must be clear. How else will she hear,

the calls of her soul Mate. The soul waits,

for no one. And that's my ideal woman.

And with this makeup, she needs no makeup. Jacob, anything designer, she's finer without those things, throw

away the ring.

Give her a crown. Let the wedding bell sound.

Cause when I meet this queen, I'm gonna marry her.

I know the fellas like Hold up, you speeding.

But this goddess deserves the Garden of Eden. A feeding,

only a king could give. We eat to live,

so long. Live my queen.

Traditional punctuations are not used. Author wants you to read the poem as if he was saying it

THOUGHTS OF A POEM

Hopefully you were inspired to write your thoughts or a poem so here's a space for you.

The Story Behind rinse cycle poem

I want to dive right into how this poem came about. It all started when I met a young lady at a poetry showcase and we ended up exchanging numbers. She expressed her admiration for my performance and asked if I could mentor her in poetry. Intrigued by her enthusiasm, I agreed to help her. During our conversations, I couldn't help but sense that she was attracted to me. It became clear that she was married, which only fueled my suspicion.

Curiosity got the best of me, and I asked her directly, "Are you married?" Her response was unexpected as she said, "Yes! If you want to call it that, but yes." Her tone conveyed a lack of respect and a desire to distance herself from her marriage.

As the conversation continued, her husband walked into the room, and she had me on speakerphone the entire time. When he inquired about whom she was talking to, she replied,

"Hunnie, remember the show I went to the other night? This is one of the poets that performed. His poetry is great, and he agreed to help me with my poetry." In that moment, I witnessed a complete 180-degree change in her demeanor. Clearly, there were interactions between her and her husband while I was on the phone, where she seemed genuinely in love with him. This contrast struck me deeply.

After her husband left, she immediately asked if I could write a poem about her. Without hesitation, I agreed. As soon as I hung up the phone, the first line of the poem came to me: "Her wash is cold, she shoulders loads of dirty clothes as if it was laundry." The next day, she called me again and shared more about her troubled relationship with her husband. It was a heartbreaking story, one that unfortunately echoes through the melanin community. This inspired me to delve deeper into the topic, researching struggling relationships, heartbreak, and the pressure to conform to societal norms. The pressure to maintain an image distorted by social media, television, and radio, dictating how a melanated woman should behave and present herself.

I decided to use a metaphorical laundry scheme throughout the poem, symbolizing the struggles and burdens she carries. I also explored the influence of role models like Cardi B and Megan Thee Stallion, who are often presented as examples for our women. I incorporated all these elements into the poem, aiming to shed light on the challenges faced by melanated women, in a Society meant to break them down with false teachings.

When I finished writing, I called her to share the poem. She eagerly asked, "Did you finish my poem?" I replied with a yes. However, when she heard it, her reaction was not unexpected. But that's a conversation for another time.

RINSE CYCLE POEM

Her wash is cold.
She shoulders the loads, of dirty clothes,
like if it was laundry.
Each garment, is a form of torment,
that she's been through. Her wash cycle menstrual,
a bloody mess.
She can't wait for laundry day, to wash the pain away.
She figures if her clothes are clean, she won't remember the dirty things.
She can only see in her dreams.
She goes to the cleaners for herself esteem.
See that dress, she puts on when she's depressed, needs to be ironed and pressed,
but don't press, the issue. The issues, is her skin tissue,
and she can't count how many times it's been through the ringer.
She's been soaked in society's confusion. Let me explain.
She's been influenced to be a bad b*t*h when she wants to be a good woman.
So she rinse and rinse, until washing doesn't make sense.
And she starts to question should she continue going to the laundromat every Sunday screaming hallelujah, paying tithes, for tide, cleaning everything but still feeling dirty on the inside.
You'd be surprised how she hides, the pain between her thighs,

in a clean outfit. She's been taught not to let the hood soften her,
so love can never be her fabric softener,
for that rough exterior. And she doesn't use a dryer.
She lets her cries, drip dries, her eyes,
is on its last cycle spin, before it starts again.
But them tears would leave her scar, and whoever would've thought
doing laundry would be this hard.

Traditional punctuations are not used. Author wants you to read the poem as if he was saying it

THOUGHTS OF A POEM

Hopefully you were inspired to write your thoughts or a poem

so here's a space for you.

The Story Behind Gate Keepers Poem

Gatekeeping is something we've seen our whole life. Whether it's at the job you work or the gang you join, it's seen in all walks of life, but it's mainly talked about in the entertainment industry. What inspired me to write this poem was my experience coming into the Atlanta poetry community, or what they would call a community. When I first hit the scene in Atlanta, I was very excited because there were a lot of poetry shows. I mean, there were 2 to 3 different poetry shows every night; what more could I ask for? I love poetry; it gives me a chance to change, impact, or enhance someone's emotions or the way they think through what I say and how I feel. So I would share my poetry with anyone who would listen. I performed my poetry in the parks, barber shops, hair salons, and nail shops all over the city every day, and I'd perform on every stage at night, so I gained notoriety very quickly.

The so-called poetry community didn't like that, and that's when their mission began. They started by trying to give me unsolicited advice. Some of the advice they gave me was that I shouldn't perform so often. They said I would burn myself out. But unlike them, I wrote poetry all the time so the audience wouldn't hear the same poems repeatedly. Plus, this was more of a ministry to me, so I had to preach the word. In my opinion, you can't speak too much life into someone. They tried to press upon me the ways they operated and told me I should do the same, not as a suggestion but as a demand. When I didn't succumb to what they wanted, they noticed I was too strong to be bullied. My poetry was too powerful to be downplayed, so they started spreading rumors that I was a troublemaker and that I hated my melanin women. I even heard a story about me snatching the mic out of someone's hand (LOL), all of which are untrue. They sent me a message by way of a poet. His words were, "We really like you. Your poetry is great, you just have to play your position get in line and do what you are told. Wait your turn. Some of us have been here ten years plus. What makes you think you can skip the line?"

Obviously, that conversation didn't end well. I wasn't the only one this happened to, but I was the only one who wasn't going to let it happen. I remember the first time I performed

"Gatekeepers"; it sent shockwaves through the poetry community, and from that moment on, they knew no gates could hold me, so their gatekeeping was useless on me.

GATE KEEPERS POEM

I'm upsetting, the settings, of the gatekeepers,
but I can care less. I'm tired So I'm gonna let these words rest,
on the ears, of those who choose to hear,
because y'all feed us, protect the fetus.
Children, are civilians, becoming casualties of war, from these gatekeepers wanting more.
Futures are becoming past without a present, and you have the nerve,
to curve, someone's creative process.
If that doesn't work you use gossip.
Spoken words impact is enormous.
You're less concerned with the words, and more with the performance.
That's why you act out.
But be warn this is not a script.
The words that come off your lips,
is someone's gospel. So be careful what you preach.
Your reach, may be long and strong, to those who are weak, but your flesh is tender in the lion's teeth.
And what you thought was sheep,
was a wolf in sheep clothing, a star unfolding.
You could have helped shape the molding.

Instead, you chose to ignore your calling, but your phone bill passed due and you got to answer.
I don't have the answers.
Just a couple of suggestions.
Kill your resting b*t*h Face, dis taste,
for everybody's art but yours.
Do it from a pure place and not just for a round of applause.
You see the Lauren Hill's and Jill's, music sends chills.
They words you can feel.
Like live for me, live for me.
Why don't you live for me, or live through me.
Discover the peace in helping someone is soothing.
Remember you was a child once, not at age, but at stage.
And it's different stages to growth, different stages to go.
I know! there's no business like show business, but whose show is this?
This gate gardening is disheartening.
You should be gardening, and harvesting.
These young voices, give them choices,
to choose not to lose, because it's a lot to lose, and there's no more better blues,
without Denzel Wesley, Dizzy Gillespie.
Let's see,
everybody win. Let everybody in.

                                        who gave you the right to choose
They say Christ died for everybody sins.

So why don't you live for me?

Traditional punctuations are not used. Author wants you to read the poem as if he was saying it

THOUGHTS OF A POEM

Hopefully you were inspired to write your thoughts or a poem so here's a space for you.

The story behind walking dead poem

I had to pick this poem to come right after Gatekeepers because their stories are connected. Very shortly after arriving in Atlanta, I found out who the so-called gatekeepers were, who the poetry community revered as the hierarchy. These poets, about four of them, were given this title by the community because they had participated in a popular TV show called "Def Poetry Jam" that aired about 20 years ago. I met these poets before I fully understood the structure of the poetry community.

As I mentioned before, I quickly made a name for myself through my work ethic and the quality of my poetry. But what I didn't know, and would later find out, was that they already knew who I was before I got to know them personally. Their first step was to try to recruit me to their team. Oh yeah, I forgot to mention this, the poetry community is full of different teams or cliques.

Throughout the process of them trying to recruit me (which I didn't realize was their intention at first, but eventually found out and declined), I spent some time around them. We had many conversations, and in most of these conversations, they would bring up "Def Poetry Jam" and how things used to be, reminiscing about their past successes and performing the same poems from 20 years ago. There were little to no discussions about their future. I could see that they were stuck in the past, chasing a high they could never experience again. They had no thoughts of reinventing themselves, believing that their best poems were behind them.

Essentially, they had become the walking dead. This happens to most of us at some point in our lives when we try to find new feelings from old things. The key to life is embracing new experiences. You'll never recapture the joy of your first party, first sexual experience, or first job because those moments came at a specific time in your life. The problem arises when you're 30 years old attending the same party you did when you were 15, seeking that same joy but unable to find it because it's gone. Now you're stuck in the past, unaware of the present, which prevents you from having a future, and you become the walking dead.

WALKING DEAD POEM

I see dead people.

Souls that have left their physical form, in the hopes of being reborn,

To their past life.

with a chance to get what they once had.

It's up for grabs, will sell their soul for the bag.

Dreams of happier days, but without direction and path, it could make a person enraged,

To the point where they kill themselves become the walking dead, and negativity and hatred, is which their energy

Is fed.

They feed on all around and in their regrets and failure they will drown.

And before the funeral, there's a public viewing, of them stewing,

in their past accomplishments.

Recalling deceased memories. And the future becomes a enemy.

And you can smell their rotten corpse, of loss,

despair, fear. Let me pour some out for my homies who are not here,

but are standing right here.

In memory, of those deceased from living in memories,

Death of the past, living life in a cast,

a shell of themselves.

So as we all gather here today, to send these lost souls away, does anyone have something to say?

Yes.

If you haven't guessed,

What I have to say, this poem is about people who never see the sunrise cause they're too busy living in yesterday.

> Traditional punctuations are not used. Author wants you to read the poem as if he was saying it

THOUGHTS OF A POEM

Hopefully you were inspired to write your thoughts or a poem so here's a space for you.

The story behind God's Words poem

This is one of my poems that didn't stem from interaction with a specific person. This poem emerged from deep soul-searching. I threw many questions into the Universe, and the answers I received formed this poem. My first question was: why does society want to convince us that we're black? The truth is, very few of us are truly the color black. There are countless shades and colors of melanin. My second question was: why are we hated worldwide despite our immense contributions to humanity?

Well, through my research and personal belief, I came to this conclusion. The reason they insist on us identifying as black is to further distance us from our true selves. Our identity has been erased and replaced. That's actually a line from one of my poems, but moving forward, I firmly believe that we are the true children of Israel and that the stories in the Bible were about us and for us. There's a quote in the Bible that I'm paraphrasing, but it says, "Ye are gods, but when you break the commandments, you die as mere mortals."

So, they blind us with distractions covered in sin, keeping us in ignorance so that we can never reach our full potential. We are the only people who possess what they call the "god gene." We are the only people who carry every element of the earth within our DNA. That's why every race hates us, because they know who we truly are. What's sad is that we don't know who we are. Hence, my opening line in the poem is, "Who do you think you are?" This question is directed at my people and also represents the sarcastic inquiry we face when we have knowledge of self—when we embrace our true identity.

The poem serves as the answer for both scenarios. That's why I conclude the poem by stating, "I am," which is the most powerful statement known to man because we are the most powerful statement known to mankind.

GODS WORDS POEM

Who do you think you are?

I am a star glazing for all to see.

Those without self knowledge fear me.

    Who do you think you are?

I am what the 1% which they represent.

I am what money cannot buy.

I am a soul tied, to the most high.

    Who do you think you are?

Well, they call me black, but in fact,

I am the sky the ground, every compound,

and molecule that makes the universe,

I am earth, wind and fire.

I carry the blood of the true messiah.

    Who do you think you are?

I am.

Every frequency, food for thoughts, so come and eat with me.

*I **am** the recipe.*

Who do you think you are?

*I **am** a celestial being, which is more than a human being. My celestial dreams,*

are manifestations.

*I **am** the world's hardest math equation. I **am** the true Asian.*

*I **am** the original Native American, and the earth is my inheritance.*

Who do you think you are?

*I **am** what they studied but don't understand, the truth question is how can God fit inside of a man?*

*I **am** first I am last. I am the future I'm the past.*

*I **am** the reason nature behaves.*

*I **am** a creature that never age.*

*I **am** every stage, of everything.*

*I **am**.*

Traditional punctuations are not used. Author wants you to read the poem as if he was saying it

THOUGHTS OF A POEM

Hopefully you were inspired to write your thoughts or a poem so here's a space for you.

The story behind Manifestation poem

This poem is just what the title says. However, it didn't start off like that. It wasn't even supposed to be a manifestation poem. When I began writing poetry, I was in a small town in Greensboro, North Carolina during the COVID-19 pandemic. Most businesses were closed or had restrictions, so I had limited places to perform. Someone told me about Instagram Live and their poetry shows, which had open mic's. Over the next couple of months, I went live on Instagram and performed day and night. During this time, I found myself battling with a poetry group called The Deadly Pens.

I started this poem in retaliation to a poem written about me. The original name of this poem was "Life Without Ink," in contrast to their name being "The Deadly Pens." Hence, why the poem starts the way it does. In the beginning, before the world started spinning, God painted a masterpiece. He completed a portrait of a fortress without any ink. What started off as an attack turned into a beautiful message for the world to hear. God works in mysterious ways. We have been taught to put limitations on who we are and what we can do—it's hard to believe, but trust me, it's true. Just listen to your everyday sayings, such as "I'm only human" or "I'm not perfect." How are you not perfect? God's creation is perfect, and you are part of it. We've been taught to dumb down our power of manifestation and call it luck. You can will anything into existence, especially through the power of words.

Words are powerful and the oldest thing in existence. Let me end by quoting the Bible: "In the beginning was the Word."

MANIFESTATION POEM

At the beginning, before the world start spinning,
god painted a masterpiece. He completed a portrait of a fortress without any ink.
His manifestation was our creation.
That's how the mind works with no limitation.
Great thought of the Divines, mind, is mines, cause great minds, think a like.
And within that portrait, he left a copy of itself. I am he If no one else.
before there were books on the shelf, Proverbs was words, that were spoken to describe the native land, origin of man.
Point of origin.
Directions, navigated by the stars reflection, X in,
the galaxies orbit. In tune, with Luna's Moon. A monsoon,
of imagery, Ink. Is the inn me.
So when I bleed, it's a masterpiece. My blood brings peace,
to a revolution of thought.
Concentration, is a form of manifestation.
That's how man feeds a nation.
Food for thought, substance is lost.
When we put value to paper.
The physical, is an individual, but the mind is one.

And the minute we realize that manifestation is everything, the mind has won.

Traditional punctuations are not used. Author wants you to read the poem as if he was saying it

THOUGHTS OF A POEM

Hopefully you were inspired to write your thoughts or a poem so here's a space for you.

The reason for the story and what was happening while the story was being told

To ask why I wrote this book is to ask why I write poetry. It's a release, and it gives me a chance to explain that release. I actually started a book shortly after writing my first three poems. However, the book was put on hold due to court proceedings for false charges I was facing. With that going on, along with shooting my documentary and living out of my van, I had no time or energy for the book, so I shelved the project.

Fast forward, my court case is over, I've moved to Atlanta, and I'm hosting poetry events and saying poetry every day to sell my merchandise, and plus because I love it. I'm knee-deep into my documentary, which is shot, edited, and ready to go at this point, but on hold as we wait for a network to buy it. There were also some suspicious mishaps and inconsistencies with the LLC for the movie on my partner's behalf. But I won't get into that at this time. So, with the documentary on hold and the story of poetry still untold, was my inspiration to write a book.

The reason for the movie was to spread my message worldwide, so the book will take on that mission. It took me approximately three weeks to write the book. I came up with the concept of adding a story to each poem while helping and teaching a young poet how to sell her book. She had a book full of poetry, and she explained to a customer that each poem would tell how she felt and what she was going through. That's when the idea came to me to tell the story of how each poem came to life after every poem in the book.

It was like a pregnancy; something was growing inside me. Every day, it would get bigger and bigger until one day it finally came out. I sat on the idea for about a week before I started writing, using the excuse that I didn't have a notebook or a pen. A bit of advice, be careful with excuses, because you might find one you like, and then love and eventually married then it's till death do you part. But then, one day, as I was putting some stuff away in my room, the thought came to me to start writing the book. Immediately, the excuses followed, saying I didn't have a pen or notebook. But as I picked up a bag off the chair, there, like magic, was a pen and a pad.

God knows how many more weeks I would have procrastinated if that didn't happen. I believe I wanted it bad enough, and my power of manifestation kicked in. Once I started writing, I couldn't stop, though I had to take breaks for stage performances and selling merch. After one day of writing the book, I called the young lady who designed flyers for my shows and asked if she could make the cover for my book, and she said yes. I was about five poems into my book when I started doing heavy research into self-publishing, which helped me put a budget together. My budget was $2,600, but I had a negative balance of $3,600.

Let me explain how I got here. I've mentioned before that I am a full-time poet, and this is my sole source of income. If I'm not selling merchandise, I'm not making money. I devoted 70 percent of my time and earnings to my documentary. The money spent and time required for the documentary depleted my funds. Essentially, I was living day to day and always a month behind. But I had this powerful message to deliver through my book, and not having enough funds to complete the self-publishing process wasn't going to stop me. If there's a will, there's a way. My next thought was to try to get a loan or an investor, a helping hand like my poem. I started with my family, putting together a proposal detailing what the book was all about.

To the best of my knowledge, there hasn't been a book done like this before. A reminder of my track record as a great salesman laid out a strategy for marketing the book. It showed that within the first two weeks of the book being released, they could see a return on their investment.

Mind you, I made it clear I wasn't asking for the whole amount; it was whatever they could afford. I heard 'no' in every language from my family, and with such anger behind it. That made me curious, so I asked a question. "If I die, would ya'll pay for the funeral?" The answer was yes. They said they would, as they would have no choice. The sad thing is, my family and most families in urban communities would rather spend $10,000 on a funeral instead of investing that money into someone's life.

However, I did have one family member who was very supportive of my poetry throughout. My big brother, Happy, actually invested $100.00 into my book. The next step was to call everyone I knew. Only one person chose to invest: a friend of mine named Donta. He invested $50.00. There were people who I contacted that just didn't have it, and I understand that.

Behind on my rent, living day to day, and only having a very small portion of the budget needed to self-publish the book, I had to make a decision. I could either continue to live day by day and a month behind, or take a leap of faith and put everything on the line. I decided not to pay the rent and put every single dollar into getting my book published, even at the risk of being homeless. I felt so alone at this point, but I knew I had a mission that needed to be fulfilled. It was time to get dirty, and I mean get it out of the mud. But the sad thing is, I'm no stranger to this. I've done it my whole life. So, I went into an overtime hustle, but when it rains, it pours. I mean, literally, every day for 5 to 6 hours of the day, it would be a thunderstorm with harsh rainfall.

At this point in my life, I didn't own a car, so you can see how the rain kind of handicapped me. On top of that, I sprained my knee, and don't ask me how because I don't know. What I do know is that I went to the emergency room, and the doctor suggested that I rest for 3-4 days for it to heal. But that wasn't an option. I had no time to rest. With the bad weather, bad knee, and a lot of stress, I had no choice but to go to war. I had to fight the temptation of letting these obstacles stop me. So, I laced up my boots and hit the streets.
I'm not going to lie, I felt a little discouraged at first, but when I hit the street and saw how my poetry changed people's lives, that gave me all the power I needed. It was as if I had already made the money for the book. I could envision book signings as if they had already happened.

At that very moment, I could hear the voices of people my book had impacted. This made me push harder. I hustled my merchandise like never before. I noticed that after two days, it stopped raining, and my knee injury had healed. Walking strong on faith took a ton of weight off my shoulders, and everything started to align. My thoughts were clear, so clear I came up with the idea to sell space in my book for sponsors.

Things were going well, so well in fact, that some of the people I had previously called to invest called me back and were interested in investing. So, in just a week after lacing up my boots and hitting the pavement, I went from negative to positive. I mean that in two ways. Let me explain. I told y'all I was discouraged the first day I went out. I felt I had no help, and no one believed in me. But I was reminded of my purpose by the people, and that changed my mindset, from negative to positive, which took me from negative $3,600.00 to only $1,000.00 away from my goal.

I tell you, life is poetic. There's a poem for every situation you go through. Tell it and move to the next poem, and hopefully, you can help someone learn from your mistakes or be empowered by your success. Thank y'all for reading. I hope y'all enjoyed and learned from this experience. Be sure to turn to the next page and get a sneak peek at part two of this book. See you in the sequel!

Sneak peek introduction the sequel

Welcome to the sequel. Reading this lets me know you enjoyed part one, but part two is a whole different monster. The bulk of the poems in this book were banned from social media because they didn't fit the agenda pushed by society today. With a deeper dive into how the poems were made, these stories are mind-blowing and controversial. My life is a movie, and each poem is an epic scene from that movie. The sequel deals with a wider range of topics, from slavery to politics, transgender issues, even COVID, and so much more. You won't believe the stories that sparked these poems. Experience is the best teacher, but reading about those experiences is one hell of a classroom.

THE END

www.ingramcontent.com/pod-product-compliance
Lightning Source LLC
Chambersburg PA
CBHW070735230426
43665CB00016B/2245